CW0057113

STANIER 8F
2-8-0

STANIER 8F

2-8-0

A STUDY OF THE STANIER LMSR CLASS 8F LOCOMOTIVE

edited by

KEITH TYLER   JOHN BOND   ALAN WILKINSON
FOR THE STANIER 8F LOCOMOTIVE SOCIETY LTD

D. BRADFORD BARTON LIMITED

Frontispiece: Class 8F 483339 (H44) approaches Chinley on a routine mineral empties working after a stiff climb from the Cheshire plain. Stanier's standard 2-8-0 class proved to be a valuable contribution to the development of freight locomotive design in this country. The story of its numerous members is unusual, and in some respects unique. Over the years they established an enviable reputation as sturdy, reliable locomotives, thoroughly suited to the work they were designed to perform.

[A. Tyson]

Identification

The following code is used to identify locomotive works and building dates:

A : Ashford	B : Brighton	BP : Beyer Peacock Limited
C : Crewe	D : Darlington	Dn : Doncaster
E : Eastleigh	NBL : North British Locomotive Co. Ltd.	
S : Swindon	VF : Vulcan Foundry Limited	H : Horwich

thus (C42), for example, indicates "Built Crewe works 1942".

other abbreviations are:

ESR : Egyptian State Railways	ISR : Iran State Railways
TCDD : Turkish State Railways	RE : Royal Engineers
WD : War Department	

Bibliography

Various issues of *The Engineer, The Locomotive, Railway Carriage and Wagon Review, The Railway Gazette* and *The Railway Magazine* 1935/44: also *The Railway Observer* and the Journal of the Stephenson Locomotive Society 1935/44 et seq.

The Railway Publishing Co. *(The Railway Gazette)—British Locomotive Types*— (for weight diagram, leading dimensions and other data).

E. S. Cox—*Locomotive Panorama* vol. 1

E. S. Cox—*British Railways Standard Steam Locomotives*

O. S. Nock—*Sir William Stanier; an Engineering Biography*

A. J. Powell—*Living with London Midland Locomotives*

Brian Haresnape—*Stanier Locomotives*

J. W. P. Rowledge—*Engines of the LMS Built 1923-51*—(for details of the complicated numbering sequence, including overseas)

Railway Correspondence and Travel Society—*The 2-8-0 and 2-10-0 Locomotives of the War Department*

C. I. Savage—*History of the Second World War: Inland Transport*

The Railways of Persia—reprinted from the *Railway Gazette* of 3rd October 1941

British Work on Persian Railways—reprinted from the *Railway Gazette* of 2nd and 16th February 1945

R. M. Robbins—*190 in Persia. Some Notes on a War-time Railway Operation*

The Royal Engineers Journal, March 1953

Various issues of *The Sapper* over the period of overseas military operation of Stanier 8Fs and at Longmoor

D. W. Ronald and R. J. Carter—*The Longmoor Military Railway*

R. Tourret—*War Department Locomotives*

J. W. P. Rowledge—*Heavy Goods Engines of the War Department* vol. 2, Stanier 8F 2-8-0

The Times Atlas of the World— (place names in the text are as in use at the time; names in brackets are the equivalent used in this atlas where they are substantially different)

© *copyright D. Bradford Barton*   IRRC   785/2 PN   *ISBN 0 85153 283 7*

printed in Great Britain by H. E. Warne Ltd, London and St. Austell

for the publishers

D. BRADFORD BARTON LTD · Trethellan House · Truro · Cornwall · England

introduction

Sir William Stanier designed his standard 2-8-0 heavy freight locomotive as an integral part of his motive power re-equipment of the London, Midland & Scottish Railway in the nineteen thirties. The class was destined to fulfil a very much wider role than this however, and ultimately its members contributed a distinguished chapter to railway history, in many ways unique. They were compact for their power and arguably the best looking of all freight locomotives. We trust that this book, the first devoted solely to the remarkable story of the Stanier 8Fs, will prove to be a worthy tribute to a robust and outstanding design.

The first modern heavy freight locomotive in this country was Churchward's fine 28xx class for the Great Western Railway, introduced in 1903, the first 2-8-0 design for British use. Stanier brought to the LMS all the major precepts of Churchward boiler and mechanical design, and improved on these to produce—among other excellent machines—a thoroughly versatile freight locomotive. The wartime Austerity 2-8-0 was a direct adaptation of the Stanier 8F, simplified for large scale production in the face of competing armaments demands for skilled labour and materials: from this was developed the Austerity 2-10-0, which in turn formed the model for the excellent British Railways 9F 2-10-0. The Stanier 8F may therefore claim to occupy a key position in this mainstream line of British freight locomotive development.

When the Stanier 2-8-0s appeared in 1935, the heaviest freight duties on the LMS were handled by 0-8-0 class 7F locomotives and a small number of Beyer-Garratts. LNWR types—the Super Ds—were predominant and by far the most successful; the equivalent Fowler engines were let down, like other designs from the same source, by inadequate bearing surfaces. The Stanier 2-8-0 gave an immediately obvious advance on these 7F predecessors in reliability as well as giving better riding, and the considerable increase in drawbar horsepower enabled significantly heavier trains to be run at higher speeds. The free-running capabilities of the 8Fs were quickly recognised; they performed well over the whole range of freight duties, tackling express goods and parcels trains with ease, and comfortably handled passenger work in emergencies where speeds in the sixties were recorded. The relationship of eight-coupled 4ft 8½in driving wheels to two 18½in × 28in cylinders with 10in diameter long travel valves, a well proportioned free-steaming boiler and excellent front-end design, allied to an all up weight in working order of 125.75 tons, of which some 63 tons were available for adhesion, and producing a tractive effort of 32,438 lbs, proved to be a very sound one; these engines were found to be equally at home slogging up to Peak Forest with 1,000 tons of limestone or hustling a load of excursionists towards the Fylde Coast, while on at least one occasion in the summer of 1955 two of the class were entrusted with the Royal Train between Aberystwyth and Milford Haven, becoming as a result of that duty the only two to be fitted for train steam heating.

Freight locomotives commonly survive longer than their racier counterparts; consequently, with no initial need for rapid replacement of existing LMS freight locomotive stock, only 126 8Fs had been built by 1939. The outbreak of war brought a dramatic change however: as the Stanier engines were thoroughly proven, and at that time the best choice available, the design was selected by the War Department as its standard locomotive for overseas service. In all, 208 were built to Ministry of Supply order for the WD by the North British Locomotive Company and by Beyer Peacock & Company; of these, 27 NBL ones were diverted to Turkey as part of a commercial export order, while the remainder saw service with British Army units in Iran and on the Egypt/Palestine/Lebanon railway system, together with further engines requisitioned from the LMS. Many of the Iran engines worked on the formidable supply route to Russia between the Persian Gulf and the Caspian Sea, where prolonged and heavy gradients made oil firing essential. Some eventually reached Italy, where fifteen were absorbed into the stock of the State Railway after 1945, as were others in Egypt, Iran, Iraq and Israel. All these have since been replaced, but some in Turkey continue in operation, over nine years after the end of stream traction on British Rail.

At home, the Ministry of Transport, facing an increasingly serious shortage of freight locomotives in 1941/42, decided that, because of their route availability, proven performance, and reliability under adverse circumstances, only Stanier 8Fs should be built. As a result 205 more engines appeared to LMS order, while another 245 were built by the other three railway companies, emerging from Ashford, Brighton, Eastleigh, Swindon, Crewe, Horwich, Darlington, Doncaster and the North British Locomotive Company's Glasgow works between 1941 and 1945. Most of the 'foreign' built engines were loaned initially to the railway companies that constructed them, with the exception of the SR, though regarded officially as LMS stock. A further 68 engines were ordered by the LNER for its own use, and were turned out by the Southern Railway's Brighton works and the London and North Eastern Railway's own workshops: these—LNER class 06—were transferred later to the LMS as part of a standardisation measure.

Thirty nine of the WD engines returned from the Middle East in 1948 and were absorbed into BR London Midland region stock. A further three locomotives—including the preserved 8233—were taken into BR stock in 1957 following many years of military service, to give a total of 666 Stanier 2-8-0s operating in this country. Altogether 852 were built, making them the largest Stanier class, and the fourth largest class of British locomotive, their numbers being exceeded only by the Ramsbottom DX goods (943), their own Austerity counterparts (935), and the GWR 57xx and 8750 pannier tank series (863).

Stanier 8Fs penetrated almost every part of the country. From their introduction they dominated freight operations on the heavily used Midlands lines until replaced by diesels in 1965/66. During the war they operated over all the Big Four railways and could be seen hauling their vital cargoes to all parts of the mainland. In BR days the majority worked on London Midland region, but allocations to the Eastern, North Eastern, Western and Scottish regions meant that they could be seen as far north as Perth, eastwards to March and Norwich, westwards to Plymouth and southwards to Bournemouth or Southampton. As dieselisation progressed, they became confined to the north western lines of the LM region, where they played a memorable part in the last days of steam traction.

These final years saw degeneration towards grimy, soot encrusted locomotives, frequently run down, but which—when resolutely handled—could still vividly revive memories of halcyon days. Throughout the last summer of steam and right into the final hours Stanier 8Fs remained hard at work on what were often 'top link' freight duties: indeed when the end came in August 1968 they accounted for over half the remaining locomotives. It is not without significance that the sight of a grimy 8F leaking steam in copious quantities but still chattering violently and crisply at the chimney top typified the end of that era which began with *Locomotion* on the Stockton & Darlington Railway in 1825.

Then came preservation. The Stanier 8F Locomotive Society secured 48773 direct from BR service at the cessation of steam traction in 1968, and she now leads an active life on the Severn Valley Railway under her earlier number and livery as LMS 8233 after having run on six railways in three continents. 48431 was rescued from Barry scrapyard in 1971 and is now operating on the Keighley & Worth Valley Railway, whilst 48151 awaits restoration on the Yorkshire Dales Railway.

This volume outlines the history of this ubiquitous and deservedly popular class, and indicates its overall scale of operation. Whilst we do not claim that our account is complete, and would welcome letters from readers who can amplify the details, we have sought to convey accurately and concisely the information we have gathered from many sources, and to present the story in its true perspective. Any mistakes are our own. If you derive half as much honest enjoyment from this book as we have had in preparing it, the endeavour will have been fully justified.

A classic portrait of a classic class: 48154 (C42) at March shed in magnificent external condition, on 26 August 1958 after working in on a freight from the Midlands. The numbering sequence of the class is complicated, and made more so by numerous changes in the case of locomotives sent overseas: readers should refer to *Engines of the LMS 1923-51* by J. W. P. Rowledge for details.
[P. H. Groom]

An early construction scene at Crewe works, thought to show one of Lot 130 of 1936/37 (8012-8026). In general LMS two- and three-cylinder design under Stanier derived from the NBL-designed 'Royal Scots', though with Swindon-based axleboxes, while the boilers were developments of the immensely successful Churchward formula. By the careful design of steam passages to reduce pressure loss in the steam flow, following Swindon precedent but also benefiting from the later work of Chapelon, Stanier secured maximum output from the steam generated. [British Rail]

Works photograph of 8111 (C39). By the end of 1939 57 Stanier 2-8-0s had been built at Crewe, making with the Vulcan Foundry engines a total of 126. This was a relative trickle compared with the flood to come when the design was produced by the majority of the principal locomotive works in the country. [British Rail]

The first twelve locomotives were built at Crewe with a shorter firebox, domeless boiler and regulator in the smokebox, and were rated 7F until the advent of the later standard Stanier boiler fitted to 8012 onwards. Initially these early engines were not vacuum train brake fitted. A further difference between these twelve and the rest was the fork-ended combination lever of the former. Detailed design on the early Black 5s and 8Fs was done at Horwich, and this small feature appears to be a legacy from the Horwich 'Crab'. 8000 here approaches Elstree on a northbound train of coal empties. These first twelve engines were all turned out with Mark I 4000 gallon rivetted tenders.

[C. R. L. Coles]

Works photograph of 8042 (VF36) with a Mark II welded tender. The Vulcan Foundry built 69 Stanier 2-8-0s in 1936/37 under Lot 132. [National Railway Museum]

Mother and daughter, both Swindon built: 2857 (S18) and 48444 (S44) at Newton Abbot. The Stanier design derived from the 28xx very much as the Black Five derived from the 'Hall'. Churchward's use of Stephenson valve linkage, though heavier and with greater frictional losses, reduced compression at very low speeds and together with a slightly greater tractive effort of 35,380 lbs compared with 32,438 lbs gave the 28xx an edge in low speed haulage of very heavy mineral trains. The Stanier design with its Walchaerts linkage ran very freely at speed and, with its higher drawbar horsepower, had an advantage in hauling express freights. 2857 is preserved on the Severn Valley Railway. [R. C. Riley]

Ex-L N W R Super D 9352 and 8006 (C35) heading north towards Bushey with empty coal wagons. In 1929 the LMS built thirty 40T capacity bogie hopper wagons of the type shown here specifically to carry fuel to the LMS power station at Stonebridge Park, which supplied electricity for the electric suburban services of north and west London. Note that the 8F is now vacuum train brake fitted. [LCGB—Ken Nunn Collection]

8033 (VF36) on a typical pre-war mixed freight on the former Midland lines, heading for Nottingham. The 8Fs rapidly established a lasting reputation for reliability and good steaming, for this reason becoming popular with footplatemen and traffic control alike. There were hazardous and adventurous days ahead for locomotives of this class, when wartime stresses conscripted them for arduous and invaluable service at home and overseas in much harsher climes. [C. R. L. Coles]

Of what 8Fs were regularly capable is clearly seen in this view of 8080 (VF36) thundering through Marley near Keighley with a northbound fully fitted freight from Leeds, heading for the assault on 'the Long Drag' to Carlisle over Ais Gill. This photograph captures all the power and vigour of these fine locomotives. [Eric Treacy]

8310 (C43) was one of the engines built under the authority of the wartime Railway Executive Committee of the Ministry of Transport, seen here with Mark II 4000 gallon welded tender. It was at about this time that a minor design change was made resulting in a straight instead of a curved reversing rod. As she stands over the ashpits, her shimmering plating is in spotless workaday contrast to the all too frequently run down external condition to become typical in the later war years, and indeed in later BR days in the face of ever rising running costs and staff shortages.

[C. R. L. Coles]

Works photograph of 8600 (E43), the first of 105 Stanier 8Fs to be constructed in 1943 and 1944 by the Southern Railway to the order of the Railway Executive Committee. The order was fulfilled by Eastleigh with 23, Ashford with 14 and Brighton with 68.

[British Rail]

L N E R 7675 (B44) was the last of 25 engines built at Brighton works to the order of the L N E R—class 06. This engine became 3124 (1946) and 3524 (1947) in later renumbering schemes. It subsequently became L M S 8729 when the L N E R, having acquired ex-W D Austerity 2-8-0s from the Ministry of Supply after the war, rationalised their stock by taking further Austerity 2-8-0's from the L M S in exchange for their Stanier engines. Another 43 engines were built at Darlington and Doncaster to the order of the L N E R in 1945 and 1946.

[National Railway Museum]

Works photographs of 8500 (D44) and 8510 (Dn43)—two of the 60 locomotives built in L N E R works from 1943 to 1945 to the order of the Railway Executive Committee, 30 each at Doncaster and Darlington. All were provided with Mark I rivetted tenders, but with L N E R standard disc wheels. Note the minor detail difference on the Doncaster engines—the prominent rivet heads on the driving wheel balance weights of 8510.

[National Railway Museum]

8400 was the first of eighty Stanier 8Fs built by the Great Western Railway at Swindon to the order of the Railway Executive Committee between 1943 and 1945: these engines were provided with Mark I rivetted and welded tenders. These photographs show details of the cylinders and motion, and will be of interest to modellers. The high standard of finish apparent here was typical of these works, though it should be added that some of the Vulcan Foundry machines were turned out with what appeared to be burnished wheel rims—a fine looking bit of extravagance that was never perpetuated in service. [British Rail]

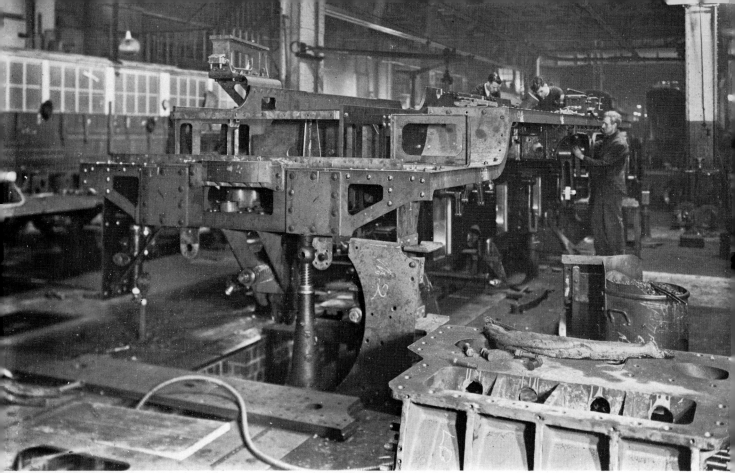

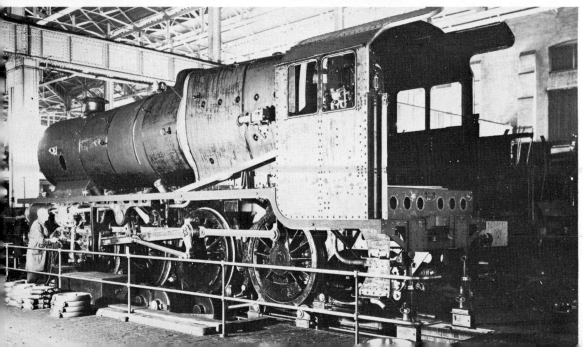

Another locomotive of
this batch on the valve
setting machine at
Swindon works. Note
the stock of eccentric
straps for the standard
GWR Stephenson valve
linkage in the
foreground.

[British Rail]

This view of an 8F under construction in Swindon 'A' shop shows the massive construction of the steam locomotive frame. Though partially stiffened by the boiler it had to resist piston thrusts of over 20 tons and a lateral bending moment approaching 120 tons ft. A cylinder casting can be seen in the foreground.   [British Rail]

A scene of well organised chaos: a general view of 8Fs under construction in Swindon 'A' shop. Note the hydraulic rivetter hanging from a crane and the various piles of components lying about, including motion brackets, cylinders with and without lagging, frame cross braces, smokebox saddle and front box member, etc. For a modeller there is an uncanny resemblance to an exploded kit assembly diagram, which of course is very much what it amounts to! Also visible are some G W R locomotives and separated pannier tanks, and what appears to be a naval gun.
[British Rail]

This illustration of an oil-fired locomotive prepared for Army service overseas, one of 51 requisitioned from the LMS, can be compared with the photographs earlier in the book. The more obvious features of this version are the cowcatcher and Westinghouse brake equipment, plus the oil tank in the tender. Unlike the locomotives previously prepared for service in France, these engines retained vacuum brake equipment. [British Rail]

D 300 (NBL40) was the first locomotive built to Ministry of Supply order for the War Department. A total of ⅜ were produced for the WD in 1940/43, 158 by the North British Locomotive Company and 50 by Beyer ₐcock and Company. Initially these engines were intended for service in France and were built to a special ₐcification including provision of Westinghouse brake equipment and wheel tyres to French profiles. However ₙe could be landed before France fell, and these, with the initial subsequent production, were given LMS ₘbers and lent to the LMS and GWR until recalled for service in the Middle East at the end of 1941. [Mitchell Library, Glasgow]

ᵥenty-seven of these engines were diverted to Turkey to fulfil commercial contracts placed in Great Britain by ᵉ Turks before the war. By arrangement with the government and as a result of various pressures the Turks were ₑntually offered Stanier 8Fs in lieu, and were well pleased with them: a relatively easy conversion to right hand ᵥe was made. Some of these locomotives survive in operation to the present day: the Turks call them ₕurchills'. The one shown here as WD 358 became TCDD 45154. [Mitchell Library, Glasgow]

Representative builders plates: top left, from LMS 8621, later BR 48621 (brass); centre left, from GWR-built engine, number unknown (brass); bottom left, from WD 438 (brass)—this engine ran as ISR 41.179 in the military operation in Persia, later became WD 70438 in the Suez Canal Zone and finally BR 48290 in September 1949 (brass); top right, from LMS 8187, later BR 48187 (brass); centre right, from LNER 3127, later LNER 3527 and LMS 8733 to become BR 48733 (brass); bottom right, from LMS 8522, BR 48522—this engine did not run under an LNER number (cast iron). Plates not shown here include 'LMS built Crewe', Vulcan Foundry 1936 and 1937, 'LNER built SR'—similar to top left, LNER plates simply stating 'built by', and 'LMS built Horwich'. [J. P. Bond]

The cab layout of the standard Stanier 2-8-0s was virtually identical to that of the Black Fives and Jubilees. The cab of an Army oil-fired engine, shown here, does have several features not found in the more usual type: noteworthy are the Westinghouse brake valve under the left hand side cab window, and the set of valves on an auxiliary steam manifold above and to the right of the firebox door for the purpose of regulating steam to various parts of the oil supply system, either for heating—a heavy oil was used—or for various burner control or cleaning functions. Below the manifold and to the right of the firebox door can be seen the operating handle for the oil supply control valve. Note also the peephole in the firebox door, which latter is only operable for maintenance. [National Railway Museum]

L M S
BUILT
1943
S R

NORTH BRITISH LOCOMOTIVE COY LTD
1942
No 24760
HYDE PARK
WORKS
· GLASGOW ·

L M S
BUILT
1944
G. W. R.

BUILT BY AND ON LOAN TO
LONDON NORTH
EASTERN RAILWAY Cº
1945
DARLINGTON WORKS Nº 1969

BEYER, PEACOCK & Cº LD
7018
MANCHESTER 1941

BUILT BY AND ON LOAN TO
LONDON NORTH
EASTERN RAILWAY Cº
1944
DONCASTER WORKS Nº 1970

The Doncaster origin of LMS 8517 (44) is evident here in the casting of the smokebox numberplate as she trudges through Dunford Bridge in wartime on the LNER/Great Central route from Sheffield to Manchester via Woodhead: plans for electrification had at that time been shelved.

[H. C. Casserley]

It must give one a mental jolt to find a locomotive of such obviously Crewe outline, built at the Brighton works of the Southern Railway in 1944, bearing just visibly the legend 'L N E R' on the tender. Without seeing it, who would believe it?

[W. Potter]

Two distinctive features of the Swindon built engines were the absence of cast smokebox numberplate, the number being painted on the bufferbeam in standard G W R manner, and the fitting of dual lamp irons to take either L M S or G W R lamps. L M S 8457 (S44), on loan to the Great Western, approaches Sonning Box with a long mixed unfitted freight, heading towards London on 21 March 1946.

[M. W. Earley]

As 8453 (S44) cautiously approaches Cheltenham Lansdown from Gloucester with a train for the Midlands shortly before the end of the war, the protective tarpaulin between the cab roof and tender can be seen, a precautionary measure introduced early in the war to cut down the tell-tale glare from the firebox door at night.   [W. Potter]

28

In the course of the 1947 L N E R renumbering engines could often be seen carrying two numbers, the new one painted on the cabside and bufferbeam and the old one on the cast smokebox numberplate, as illustrated here by class 06 3536 (D46)—later L M S 8741—working hard at the head of a heavy loose coupled freight on the L N E R mainline. Pre-war standards were not achieved again regularly for many years after the war due to the heavy backlog of maintenance and renewal to track and rolling stock, while in many areas the inferior grades of coal available made mediocre performance too often the norm.   [Photomatic Limited]

Ahwaz, 7 June 1942: Among the last of a consignment of 143 Stanier 2-8-0s shipped to Persia, WD 544 and 547 (both NBL42) arrive by barge on the river Khavan after unloading by the Anglo-Iranian Oil Company's floating crane at Abadan. It is of interest that the quayside crane lift at Ahwaz that finally brought them ashore placed such a heavy load on the local electricity supply that the town had to be cut off during unloading operations. The engines were all given ISR numbers, these two becoming respectively 41.219 and 41.222. Eventually the former, after service in Egypt, came home in 1948 to become BR 48261, while the latter became TD 1429 on the Iraq State Railways.

Ahwaz was the southern marshalling point on the trans-Iranian railway supply route operated by the British Army from Bandar Shahpur or Khorramshahr on the Persian Gulf to Tehran, where engines operated by the Russians took over for the remainder of the journey to Bandar Shah on the Caspian Sea. Locomotive availability was poor, because of the severe effect of oil firing on superheater elements, but apart from this the Stanier engines gave an excellent account of themselves considering the appalling conditions under which they worked. [Imperial War Museum]

n full cry against the grade with a freight on the down relief line passing Berkhamsted, 8626 (B43) makes an exciting and timulating contrast with the sweltering heat of the Persian Gulf on the opposite page as her exhaust plumes vigorously into the reezing air in one of the harshest winters ever, February 1948. Below, The output of Crewe (43), Brighton (44) and Darlington (46) are represented from left to right in this group on shed at Swansea. Following Nationalisation of the railway ystem in 1948, when 40,000 was added to the numbers of former LMS locomotives as opportunity arose, new and old umbers could be seen together for some time, while in some cases old company lettering on tender sides considerably outlived he first British Railways emblem. [H. C. Casserley]

Meanwhile much had been happening overseas, and we are running ahead of our 8F story . . .

Ahwaz roundhouse in June 1942. Against tremendous difficulties a weekly total of some 12,000 tons of supplies were moved north to Tehran under the direction of three Railway Operating Companies, Royal Engineers, with various supporting units, including a Railway Workshop Company situated at Tehran, who together had achieved a roughly eight-fold increase in the tonnage moved along this route. Combined with considerable lorry borne traffic this constituted a vital supply link to Russia parallel to the Arctic convoys. [Imperial War Museum]

7 June 1942: WD 507 (NBL41)—ISR 41.190—newly prepared for traffic at Ahwaz depot following delivery, in the care of a happy group of RE operating personnel. In 1944 the Russia supply operation in Iran was taken over by the US Army Transportation Corps using diesel locomotives, and the Stanier engines were dispersed. 50 were transferred to Suez or Jaffa to be overhauled for service in the Middle East or Italy: the others were eventually absorbed in Persia or Iraq. 507 went to Egypt (WD 70507) where it was acquired by the ESR in 1948 and numbered 847.
[Imperial War Museum]

WD 437 and 442 (both BP41)—respectively ISR 41.177 and 41.180—in charge of the Up Mail at Parandak, about 50 miles from Tehran on the Tehran-Ghom (Qom) section of the trans-Iranian railway in August 1942. Much of the railway and many installations, for example this station building and the Ahwaz roundhouse, were newly built just before the war. The route mileage of the British sector of operations was 576 miles (927km). 437 later reached Italy with the British Army, where it was acquired by the Ferrovie della Stato in 1946 and renumbered 737.004. 442 later went to Egypt (WD 70422), returning to Britain in 1948 to become BR 48292 in 1949. Below, WD 521 (NBL41)—ISR 41.238—and WD 600 (VF36)—ISR 41.183—at the head of a down Polish special ready to leave Arak for Ahwaz in August 1942. A long stretch south through mountainous country lies ahead, with a ruling gradient of 1 in 66. Many trains took part in the evacuation of tens of thousands of Poles of all ages released from internment by the Russians that year: those of military age formed units in the Middle East from which the Polish Corps in Italy was later drawn; civilians went mostly to camps in Palestine and East Africa, while some reached India. WD 521 later went to Palestine (WD 70521) and was acquired by the Israel State Railways in 1948 after the evacuation of British forces. WD 600 had been LMS 8048: it remained in Persia and was eventually taken into ISR stock. [E. J. M. Hayward]

199 Railway Workshops RE, Jaffa, in 1946: this was set up to repair engines running on the Palestine and Lebanon railways. WD 70579 (C37), ex-LMS 8020, WD 579 (1941) and ISR 41.151 (1941), became BR 48020 in 1949. During and after the war, until the British evacuation of Palestine, there was a large military railway network serving what was in effect a vast military base, created largely by running powers over existing state railways, extending from the deep water docks south of Suez to the Lebanon across the Sinai Desert. The Sinai link had been built in the 1914/18 war and the Haifa–Beirut–Tripoli section at the northern end in 1941/42. In the early phases of the North African campaign, Stanier 2-8-0s from the contingent of 42 sent to Egypt at the end of 1941 operated westward to Mersa Matruh on the ESR and reached Capuzzo, just inside Cirenaica, on the military-laid Western Desert Extension Railway which eventually reached Tobruk

[D. S. Currie

Tel Aviv, 1947: an unidentified Stanier 2-8-0 on a test run from 199 Railway Workshops at Jaffa. Terrorism was rife in the period before the evacuation of Palestine: hence the bren gun mounted on the cab roof. Among the organised terrorist groups active at this date were the Irgun Zvai Leumi and the Stern Gang.

[Major W. W. Kirby, GM]

WD 70376 and 70384 (both NBL41) awaiting repair at 199 Railway Workshops in 1946. The workshops are behind the wall on the right. The lines in the foreground run into Jaffa Station (Palestine Railways). The line in the background leads to Tel Aviv, Lydda, Ramla—junction for Gaza—and Jerusalem. These engines had both served in Persia (ISR 41.156 and 41.167 respectively); they eventually became BR 48253 and BR 48255.   [D. S. Currie]

Suez, 23 December 1947. Ex-Iran engine 41.135—previously 41.131, ex-WD 395 (NBL41), later WD 70321—hauling a mixed bag of WD industrial engines from El Quassasin Army depot into 169 Railway Workshops for overhaul. This was the locomotive repair organisation for the British Suez Canal base. The Stanier 8F became WD 506 (1952) and ultimately 893 when acquired two years later by the ESR. Note the auxiliary water tender. The diesel shunter was one of a number sold or lent to the WD by the LMS. The three steam locomotives, all of 0-4-0 wheel arrangement, were British built WD ME/LO/34 *Napoleon* constructed by Hawthorn Leslie in 1917, French built WD ME/LO/35 *Christa,* and German built WD ME/LO/23. A top feed modification was made to 8Fs in the Middle East after the war, arising from experience with dirty feed water: isolating valves were fitted between the boiler and the clack valves to enable the latter to be cleared with the engine in steam.

[D. S. Currie]

Heavy overhauls were undertaken by 169 Railway Workshops RE, Suez. The conditions under which such work was carried out is illustrated by this photograph taken in April 1948 showing a boiler being lifted. Various components have been stripped off the locomotive, including the cab and the expansion link brackets, while the details of the ashpan are not normally so readily available for inspection! Note the German prisoners of war doing most of the heavy work, some of 300 employed there at the time while awaiting repatriation. The workshops here were the southern counterpart of those at Jaffa, and, with their detachments, they serviced the whole of the British railway stock working on the Egypt/Palestine/Lebanon system. The engine is WD 70373, previously WD 576 (1941), built as LMS 8015 (C37), after requisition serving in Iran as ISR 41.151, later 41.153: in 1952 it became WD 514, and 839 when acquired by the ESR in 1954.

[D. S. Currie

Ismailiya, 24 February 1948: WD 70395 (formerly WD 321 (NBL40), LMS 8247, ISR 41.135 renumbered 41.131 (it finally became BR 48257 in 1949) halts to change pilotmen; ESR pilotmen were required for journeys on ESR metals. This was approximately the half way point on the journey from Suez to Port Said. This engine was hauling two dead Stanier 2-8-0s and two spare tenders, all for shipment back to Great Britain.

[D. S. Currie

Shipping out, Port Said, 28 February 1948. After being lifted from the quayside by the Suez Canal Company's 150-ton floating crane and taken out on Royal Engineers 'Z' craft, locomotives are being hoisted aboard SS 'Belnor' of Oslo by her own derricks. The degree of list is worth noting. 'Belnor' took 20 engines on this voyage: when the holds were full the remaining engines were loaded as fore-and-aft deck cargo either side of the ship's centreline with tenders placed athwartship on the outside. The engine on the derrick, WD 70332, had been WD 332 (NBL40), LMS 8258, ISR 41.132 and became BR 48251: the one waiting its turn, WD 70584, had been WD 506 (NBL41), ISR 41.218 and 41.216 and became BR 48263. [D. S. Currie]

WD 70320 *Lt. W. O. Lennox V.C. Royal Engineers* with a typical train of Army passenger stock on the Adabiya-Ataka military railway in 1950. The history of this engine is given opposite. It is worth noting that by this date Westinghouse brake equipment was no longer required and had been removed from the engines.

[Courtesy of
Col. G. C. L. Alexander OBE]

Terrorism at El Kantara (El Qantara). There was considerable unrest in 1951 with demands for the abrogation of the Anglo-Egyptian Treaty of 1936. The RE had their share of trouble with some 28 serious terrorist incidents to deal with in the Canal Zone. Mines were often triggered by nails inserted in the rail joints, while demolition charges were sometimes fired from small vessels—which promptly sailed away—on adjoining waterways. This victim of a mine is WD 70574 *Cpl. Leitch V.C. Royal Engineers* of 10 Railway Squadron; originally LMS 8019 (C37), it became WD 574 and ISR 41.175 in 1941: after repair it became WD 510 in 1952 but was scrapped about two years later.

[Courtesy of
Col G. C. L. Alexander OBE]

Power on parade. Locomotives and men of 10 Railway Squadron RE at Chequers Locomotive Depot, Adabiya in 1950. The slopes of Gebel Ataka can be seen in the background. The 8Fs are, left to right, WD 70320 *Lt. W. O. Lennox V.C. Royal Engineers,* WD 70387 *Cpl. W. J. Lendrim V.C. Royal Engineers,* and WD 70373 *Clr-Sgt. H. McDonald V.C. Royal Engineers.* The first of these had been WD 320 (NBL40), LMS 8243 and ISR 41.108 (1941); it became WD 501 (1952) on the Longmoor Military Railway. The histories of the other two are given elsewhere in this section.

[Courtesy of
Col. G. C. L. Alexander OBE]

Nameplate of WD 70387. Eight locomotives of 10 Railway Squadron RE were named after holders of the Victoria Cross in the Corps of Royal Engineers and one other *Sgt. J. Smith V.C. Bengal Sappers and Miners.* They were kept very well turned out in black livery with fine red lining on boiler bands. The squadron was based on the Adabiya–Ataka military railway south of Suez, which connected the deep water docks at Adabiya with the ESR system: it operated throughout the widespread British base in the Suez Canal Zone, hauling military traffic on the ESR system, including the run to El Tell el Kebir.

[Courtesy of
Col. G. C. L. Alexander OBE]

Locomotives at 400 Transportation Store Depot RE at Suez in December 1947, destined for return to Great Britain. This depot was next to 169 Railway Workshops outside Suez. The locomotives had come from Palestine and the Lebanon via the Sinai desert, from store at Sarafand (Zerifin) near Jaffa, and Azzib (Achzib) near Nahariyya, north of Acre: some had been overhauled at Jaffa before being placed in store. This small fragment of the 8F contingent in the Middle East perhaps gives some idea of the scale of operations.

[D. S. Currie]

Lying down is not always a reliable indication of simply being tired . . . On 15 December 1951 WD 70387 *Cpl. W. J. Lendrim V.C. Royal Engineers*—fresh from overhaul—formerly WD 387 (NBL41) and ISR 41.155—of 10 Railway Squadron was derailed by terrorists outside Suez oil refinery. Rerailing proved to be a considerable exercise because of the soft ground and adjacent watercourse, and a by-pass line had first to be laid. After retrieval and repair this engine became WD 503 in 1952 and ESR 834 two years later. The locomotive edging past on the diversion is WD 70516 *Cpl. J. Ross V.C. Royal Engineers* which had been WD 516 (NBL41) and ISR 41.201: it became WD 509 in 1952 and ESR 832 in 1954.

[Courtesy of
Col. G. C. L. Alexander OBE]

Going into action: WD 70516 hauling a detachment of tanks of the 4th Royal Tank Regiment from El Shallufa to Ismailiya a month later, seen here passing Moascar on the outskirts of the latter, to make a show of force at the height of the abrogation crisis. Colonel (then Major) Alexander, Officer Commanding 10 Railway Squadron RE, is driving.

[Courtesy of
Col. G. C. L. Alexander OBE]

WD 501 *Lt. W. O. Lennox V.C. Royal Engineers* receives attention on the Longmoor Military Railway; its history has already been outlined. It was returned to the United Kingdom for general overhaul at Derby in 1952, together with WD 500, 508, 511 and 512 which had been in store in Egypt. After overhaul they were stored at Longmoor because of the uncertain future of the Suez Canal Base. In 1955 WD 508 and 511 went to No. 2 Military Port at Cairnryan, and WD 500 (eventually preserved), 501 and 512 were brought into use at Longmoor: these three were sold to BR in 1957/58 and (last of the BR class number series) became 48773, 48774 and 48775 respectively after further overhaul at Eastleigh. Strangely, BR showed no interest in buying WD 508 and 511, which were scrapped in 1959 after unsuccessful attempts to find a purchaser.

[Major D. W. Ronald]

This busy scene at Willesden mpd in the middle 1960s, featuring 48739 (D45) and 48518 (Dn44) is as good a place as any to commence a review of Stanier 2-8-0 activities on British Railways—before the later term British Rail was adopted. 8Fs from Willesden, the main freight depot in the London area, worked extensively over the Western Division, onto the Midland Lines via Rugby and Leicester, and into other regions with transfer freights via the West London Line.   [P. H. Groom]

In the time honoured setting of Tring Cutting 48033 (VF36) heading north greets 48319 (C44) wheeling an up mixed freight towards the capital on the adjoining relief line on a September afternoon in 1959.

[C. R. L. Coles]

Double-heading with 8Fs was rare, but here 48129 (C41), working home to Willesden, assists Crosti-boilered 9F 92025 out of Rugby with a Toton-Willesden freight on 24 July 1958. A recurring fault on many of the Stanier 2-8-0s was a disconcerting habit of the exhaust injector 'knocking off' without warning when altering the valve setting. On a doubleheaded train this could be a bit surprising visually for the crew of the second engine.

[P. H. Groom]

When available, 8Fs were usefully employed on heavy empty stock workings from Euston up the 1 in 70 of Camden Bank to Wembley carriage sidings, notably the ultra-heavy sleeping car trains: 48351 (H44) prepares to leave the celebrated terminus with the stock of a train from Blackpool. It is a commentary on the railway scene that virtually everything in this picture, apart from the main section of the retaining wall, vanished in the rebuilding of the station at the time of electrification to Liverpool and Manchester. [Brian Morrison]

Nocturne in the Midlands. On a winter evening in 1966 three typically care-worn machines await their next turn of duty, 48680 built at Brighton (43), 48514 at Doncaster and 48375 at Horwich (both 44). It is of more than passing interest that steam locomotives, like the great sailing ships, making equally great demands on the crews handling them in their respective elements, inspired in the men who built, maintained and operated them an extraordinary degree of loyalty, devotion and respect: it can hardly be a coincidence that in both cases the work was physically demanding, calling for decisive skill and acute powers of judgement and initiative. Certainly the rewards endowed the spirit rather than the pocket! [J. B. Caldwell]

It is not always remembered that steam locomotives were generally serviced and maintained under primitive and often badly-lit conditions. This photograph typifies some of the 'better' facilities available as 8Fs lay over between duties in an LM modernised depot of the 1930s. [J. B. Caldwell]

One of the last long distance steam workings on the West Coast route was the heavy 10.30 Northwich-Whitehaven, which continued until March 1968. 48340 (H44) with over 800 tons on the drawbar, nears Winwick Junction in October 1967. Well driven under such arduous conditions—and such trains frequently loaded to over 900 tons and had to contend at times with weather of considerable severity—Stanier 8Fs really could be heard 'talking'.

[J. R. Whitnall]

Saturday afternoon bustle on a Cheshire by-way: Crewe South's recently outshopped 48505 (D44) slows for a brisk tablet exchange at Middlewich, heading the 12.25 Stanlow-Egginton Junction tanks in January 1965.   [A. Wilkinson]

The ten miles of Madeley bank presented a steady slog for steam-hauled southbound trains from Crewe. The rural calm of the Cheshire countryside is brusquely shattered as 48727 (B44) pounds away from Crewe towards Whitmore summit with freight for the Midlands in September 1960. [Derek Cross]

The long climb from sea level at Carnforth over Grayrigg to the 916′ altitude of Shap summit is generally considered to provide the climax of a journey on the West Coast route; certainly it was a real test of enginemen and their machines. 48433 (S44) is going well near the top of Grayrigg Bank with an Edge Hill–Carlisle express goods in the early 1960s.   [Eric Treacy]

The crux of the former L N W R route to Scotland was the four miles of relentless 1 in 75 from Tebay to Shap summit, and this section was for years a mecca for photographers. Perhaps the worst fault with heavily laden 8Fs was their occasional loss of adhesion on greasy metals, due to their comparatively light axleloading, and a tendency to 'pick up their wheels' on downgrades. Little risk of either here, as two 8Fs, with 48426 (S43) leading, shout a chorus of defiance at the Westmorland fells north of Tebay at the start of this stiff final section with a heavy track train for Carlisle in the summer of 1967.   [D. C. Williams]

The great output of the Nottinghamshire coalfield kept the railway, and the Stanier 2-8-0s in particular, very busy throughout the 1950s and the early 1960s. No fewer than four Class eights are seen here occupied with trip workings on the Mansfield Colliery branch in January 1959.

[J. Cupit]

The Stanier 2-8-0 was very much a Midland Lines engine, and monopolised the considerable freight traffic between London and the North Midlands, especially the Toton–Brent coal hauls. Here 48005 (C35) works hard approaching Melton Mowbray in 1957. This was one of the twelve original engines fitted with domeless boilers and smaller fireboxes. [P. H. Groom]

The characteristically neat lines and fine proportions of the Stanier 2-8-0 are shown to advantage in this profile of Saltley's 48647 (B43) heading steadily uphill out of Sutton in Ashfield with a freight for Washwood Heath. [T. E. Williams]

The 8Fs could show a good turn of speed when required, and were occasionally used on passenger turns or summer excursion workings, but seldom was greatness so summarily thrust upon one of them as on 2 July 1955 when 48266 (NBL42) was entrusted with the down 'Thames–Clyde Express' following a 'Jubilee' failure at Leicester. The train is seen rolling into Trent, the locomotive imperturbably bearing its distinguished headboard.   [J. Kent]

This calamity at Turvey in Bedfordshire resulted in the first Stanier 2-8-0 withdrawal in 1960; 48616 (B43) from Toton is being recovered after 'running out of road' with a track train.

[K. C. H. Fairey]

The Midland Railway signal box and signals contribute an element of timelessness to this view of Irchester Junction in the early 1960s as 48119 (C39) attacks the climb to Sharnbrook summit with a Toton–Brent coal train. The star on the cabside denotes that 50 per cent of reciprocating weights are balanced, a modification latterly made to most of the class to allow them to work class E express freights (55 mph maximum) more smoothly by reducing substantially both fore and aft oscillation and the 'nosing' tendency. [K. C. H. Fairey]

Storming the Lickey: 48163 (C43) and banker tackle the famous two miles of 1 in 37 with empties for Washwood Heath in October 1957. Banking here was obligatory for freight trains to avoid the risk of breakaways, and in fact it was rare for any train to ascend unassisted. Sections of the South Devon banks approach the severity of this grade but are not sustained.

[Courtesy J. R. Whitnall]

emory of the Great Central Line; following transfer to London Midland region this whole mainline was ered superfluous by rationalisation. Empty sidings indicate impending closure and dereliction as 48315 (C43) s Bulwell Common with short coal train.

[J. Cupit]

High in the Pennine fells, on the first falling grade in the 16 miles since Settle Junction, 48547 (D45) runs down from the eerie depths of Blea Moor Tunnel and crosses Denthead Viaduct at the start of ten miles of lightly graded and superbly aligned formation linking Ribblehead to Garsdale and the final rise to Ais Gill summit. Virtually contouring for this distance at an altitude of 1100', and approached from both directions by long gradients equally well laid out and nowhere exceeding 1 in 100, this former Midland Railway trunk route to Scotland remains one of the most remarkable monuments to the railway age in this country.   [H. C. Casserley]

Mainline through the Peak: the Derby-Manchester route, abounding in sharp curves, long gradients and numerous tunnels, had a formidable reputation. It was partially closed and lifted in the 1970s and hikers now walk
undisturbed where, in 1963, 48327 (C44) returning home to Heaton Mersey hammered through Chee Dale on the
long grind up to Peak Forest.   [A. Tyson]

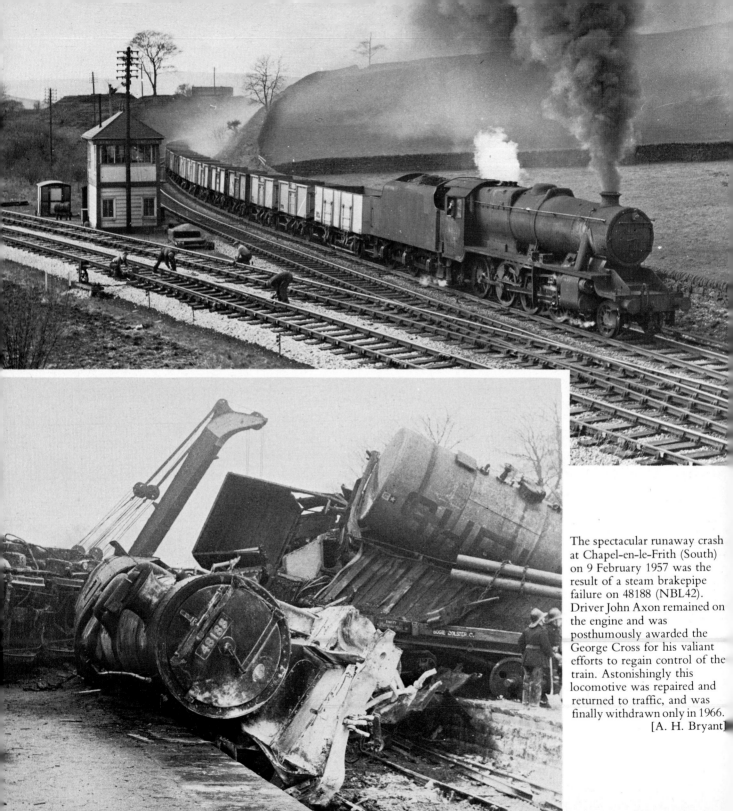

The spectacular runaway crash at Chapel-en-le-Frith (South) on 9 February 1957 was the result of a steam brakepipe failure on 48188 (NBL42). Driver John Axon remained on the engine and was posthumously awarded the George Cross for his valiant efforts to regain control of the train. Astonishingly this locomotive was repaired and returned to traffic, and was finally withdrawn only in 1966.

[A. H. Bryant]

Staveley's 48663 (B44) darkens the sky as it slams into the 1 in 100 gradient past Chinley East Junction, heading empties towards Cowburn Tunnel and through Edale into the Hope Valley on 4 April 1960, raising a cloud of dust from the lineside. [Norman Preedy]

The limestone hopper workings to Northwich from Peak Forest and Tunstead became one of the most notable regular duties of the Stanier 2-8-0s over the years, the round trip involving a prolonged climb of savage severity with the return empties and a loaded descent into the Cheshire plain with sometimes little short of 1000 tons leaning on the tender. The passage of long tunnels at Disley and Dove Holes, both on steep gradients, was conducive to a grimy appearance. 48521 (Dn44) slogs steadily up the 1 in 87 from New Mills South Junction in 1960 with a train of close-coupled vacuum-braked hoppers built for this traffic, having acquired a Fowler tender and a dent in her boiler casing. [A. H. Bryant]

Against a backdrop of factory spires, 48430 (S44) trundles a long haul of coal from the Yorkshire pits past the deserted locomotive depot at Mirfield on 18 October 1967. [Norman Preedy]

End o' t' Wakes . . . an August Saturday afternoon finds 48276 (NBL42) winding downhill from Copy Pit towards Todmorden with a Blackpool–Sheffield relief. When occasion demanded it 8Fs were perfectly capable of running freely at speeds in the upper sixties, and they could therefore cope fairly comfortably with summer Saturday timings, when their lack of train heating equipment was no disadvantage. Stability remained good at high speeds, and foot-platemen allocated an 8F could be reasonably sure of a comfortable day, which was certainly not the case with their Austerity counterparts. [R. S. Greenwood]

"Lose 'em, Mix 'em and Smash 'em" techniques in action . . . 48512 (Dn44) suffers the penalty of excess energy on as it were, the spur of the moment whilst shunting(?) at Rochdale: it is perhaps a meagre consolation that the derailed engine and wagons have had the self-respecting decency to pile up in line.   [R. S. Greenwood]

No engine is ever better than its fireman: expert wrist work with the shovel builds up the fire on 48437 (S44) for the gruelling climb ahead to Standedge summit.   [A. Wilkinson]

Fireman's view from the footplate of 48437 approaching Stalybridge with a trans-Pennine freight early in 1968. These large locomotives were as thirsty as a drayman when working hard, as many a fireman could affirm, having had to scrabble over the coals in the tender to 'put the bag in' several times during a shift: the blow-down equipment fitted may have been partly to blame, but basically it was a clear case of getting "nowt out w'owt fust puttin' summat in".   [A. Wilkinson]

In BR days 8Fs were rare in Scotland, apart from Carlisle (Kingmoor) engines working north and three stationed at Glasgow (Polmadie). Beattock bank, between the two, was a considerably more severe obstacle than Shap and demanded great staying power. In this view Kingmoor's 48758 (Dn45) breasts the last few chains to the summit on the slightly easier, though still prolonged, ascent from the north, travelling home with return empties for the south on 17 August 1960.   [P. H. Groom]

Polmadie's 48774 (NBL40) doubleheads WD Austerity 2-8-0 90549 past Terminus Junction with iron ore from Glasgow Docks to the steelworks in Lanarkshire on 26 April 1960. The Stanier engine retains its boiler with WD modified top feed, a feature seen on 48775 until withdrawn at the end of steam. Both these engines had seen service overseas, 48774 as related earlier, and 90549 on allocation to Hengelo in Holland in 1945.

[W. A. C. Smith]

First of the 'Western' class diesel-hydraulics in trouble. 48179 (NBL42), commandeered from a down freight, assists D1000 *Western Enterprise* out of Leamington for the climb of Hatton bank with a Paddington–Wolverhampton express in 1962. This diesel had a unique desert sand livery; in maroon it would have complemented the Stanier engine more appropriately—such are the hazards of unplanned double-heading. [J. R. P. Hunt]

On the Western Region, 48511 (Dn44) tops the climb out of the Severn Valley basin into the Cotswolds and emerges from Chipping Campden Tunnel with a block tank working from the West Midlands to Fawley refinery in April 1965.

[J. R. P. Hunt]

The 8Fs were frequent performers on the Paddington-Birmingham route with Nuneaton-Banbury coal trains. 48435 (S44) is working hard and steaming well as she passes Fosse Road box late on an October afternoon in 1957. The Stanier locomotive makes a pleasing contrast with the 'Castles' and 'Kings' so frequently photographed on this stretch of the Great Western route to Chester. [R. J. Blenkinsop]

The Somerset & Dorset Joint line, noted for sharp curves and severe gradients, had its own Derby-designed 2-8-0s, which were replaced by Western Region with 8Fs after 1962. 48706 (B44) here attacks the treacherous 1 in 50 out of Bath at the head of a freight for the south in October 1965. [A. Wilkinson]

The reduced allocation in the last months of the S & D meant using any locomotive that was available for passenger work. The lack of train steam heating is apparent in frosted coach windows as 48760 (Dn45) climbs smartly through Lincombe Vale with the 08.15 Bath Green Park – Templecombe on the last day of service, 5 March 1966.

[Derek Cross]

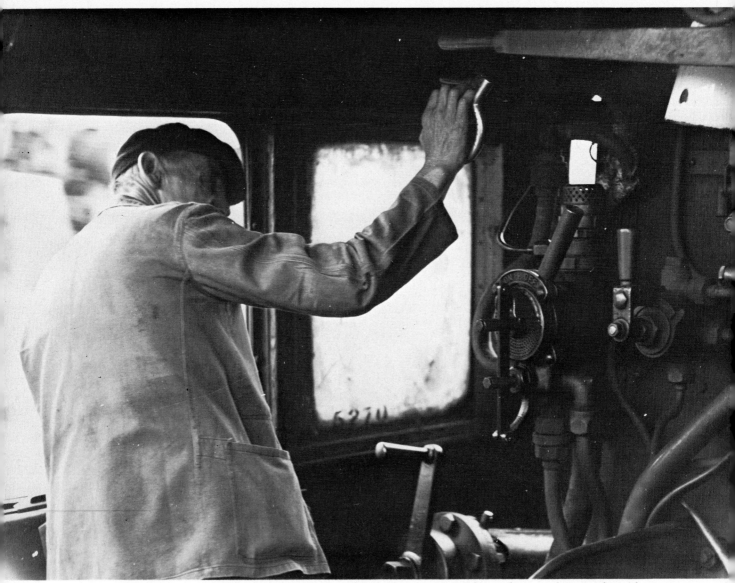

8F Engineman: Driver Burford works 48309 (C43) on full regulator and in full forward gear as she struggles with binding brakes and a 1 in 50 gradient on the climb to Masbury with an enthusiast special in April 1965. Failure to equalise air pressure completely before attaching the train to the Stanier engine after its release from a GW locomotive used on the preceding part of the journey has left some of the brakes partly 'on'. Stanier ejectors could only create a 21-inch vacuum before a reducing valve cut in, whereas Swindon ejectors created a 25-inch vacuum: this incompatibility was overcome by a modification to Stanier engines permanently allocated to Western region. (48309 was one of the two 8Fs fitted for train steam heating when modified, together with 48728 (B44), for hauling the Royal Train).

[D. H. Ballantyne]

The ex-LNWR route from Shrewsbury to Swansea took a twisting single line from Craven Arms climbing through the highlands of Central Wales. 48739 (D45) lifts a goods train bound for Swansea out of the Teme Valley and hammers up the four miles of 1 in 60 through Knucklas to Llangunllo in June 1964. Note the absence of a banking engine, and the marked effect on the train of reverse curvature.   [Derek Cross]

Old Oak Common's 48431 (S44)—now preserved at Haworth—on the 16.25 Plymouth Millbay–Paddington parcels is piloted as far as Newton Abbot by 5997 *Sparkford Hall,* seen here at Aller Junction after surmounting the ferocious South Devon banks on a summer day in 1959. The 21 Stanier 8Fs permanently allocated to Western region at this date were fitted with automatic train control equipment (precursor of the more sophisticated automatic warning system adopted later by BR), and had a modified ejector layout, entailing the fitting of a more powerful ejector mounted forward on the boiler barrel, to suit the higher operating vacuum of Western Region stock.   [C. H. S. Owen]

The Stanier 2-8-0s also played a prominent part in the heavy goods traffic on the north-east—south-west corridor. Allocated at that time to Mansfield, 48119 (C39) gets a southbound freight on the move from Dringhouses Yard, York.
[Eric Treacy]

In latter years the Southern works at Eastleigh overhauled several batches of LM Region locomotives. On 17 June 1965 48408 (S43) graduated to the 08.21 Basingstoke–Waterloo commuter service as part of a 'running-in' turn and stands at the bufferstops alongside 'Battle of Britain' light pacific 34063 *229 Squadron*, affording a rare opportunity to compare Stanier and Bulleid outlines.

[H. A. Gamble]

A fine array of upper quadrant semaphore signals frames 48622 (A43) as she heads through Church Fenton with a light express freight for the south in 1962. This type of signal, once so commonplace, has become increasingly rare with higher speeds, power box control and the general adoption of multi-aspect colourlight signalling on all main routes. [M. Mitchell]

tly to ease employment problems during the withdrawal of steam, numerous batches of LM Region locomotives were pped at 'foreign' works. 48045 (VF36) is seen at Darlington in 1965: built as LMS 8045 and commandeered in 1941 as WD 8, she ran in Iran as 41.178 and in Egypt as WD 70573, and entered BR service in 1949. Alongside stands J25 0-6-0 65033, now served. In the later fifties a large number of Stanier 2-8-0s exchanged their Stanier 4000 gallon tenders for Fowler 3500 gallon es from Jubilees, the Stanier pattern being considered more suitable for the longer non-stop runs and higher speeds of senger work. [J. R. P. Hunt]

Meanwhile Stanier 2-8-0s remained at work in several Middle Eastern countries. Israel State Railways 70510 at Haifa on 4 May 1954: this locomotive had been successively WD 510 (NBL41), ISR 41.212 and WD 70510—the Israel State Railways had taken over the WD numbering unaltered. Alongside is a class P 4-6-0 built in 1935 for the Palestine Railways by the same company.

[D. H. Ballantyne]

Iraq State Railways TD 1427 at Shalchiya Depot, Baghdad, in March 1967. The well kept appearance is noteworthy, with cast cabside numberplate, but one wonders about those very thin wheel tyres. This locomotive, WD 404 (BP40) and ISR 41.118, first ran on the GWR as LMS 8290 until recalled by the WD in 1941 for service in Persia.

[Basil Robert]

Iraq State Railways T D 1421 on station pilot duty at Baghdad West in March 1967: note the auxiliary water tender. This engine was built as WD 540 (NBL41) and ran in Persia in the British military supply operation for Russia as ISR 41.236. Stanier engines acquired by Iraq were each moved there from Iran over metre gauge lines loaded on four trolleys, coupled together.

[Basil Robert]

Iraq State Railways T E 1442 in the same location on the same day. The TE class was an interesting heavy modification of the 8F, perhaps made when new boilers were required. The Stanier chassis remains recognisable despite modified slide bar design, which was doubtless better in that sandblown environment. Note the re-use of the Stanier chimney. This engine's history is difficult to trace, but it would have started as a WD engine in the Persian operation.

[Basil Robert]

Standing alone in the huge, dimly lit cavern of Manchester Victoria, 48609 (E43) quietly sets the stage for the last act of the steam traction drama. Elimination had begun with an orderly and decisive operation throughout the west, other regions completing withdrawal more gradually, but none the less ruthlessly. There had been some brief reprieves while troubles with the largely unproven diesel fleets were brought under control, but now, with less than a year to go, attention is focused entirely on north-west England . . .   [J. B. Caldwell]

"There was a rocky valley . . . divine as the vale of Tempe; you might have seen the Gods there morning and evening . . . You enterprised a railroad . . . blasted its rocks away . . . And now every fool in Buxton can be at Bakewell in half an hour, and every fool in Bakewell at Buxton." The idiotic hustle John Ruskin feared is gently smothered by the blanketting snow in Ashwood Dale as 48117 (C39) climbs steadily to Buxton on a Gowhole tripper, her arching exhaust dispersing slowly among the frost-taut trees. Her clear cut sound, heard well before and long after she is in sight, strongly punctuates the spellbound stillness of the valley, where every footfall crunch intrudes and the crack of a twig is etched on silence . . . February 1968.

[J. R. P. Hunt]

Final years of grime, grit and neglect: 48272 (NBL42) has made her last run and is cooling down on Northwich depot: ordered as WD 559, she was loaned to the LMS when newly constructed as 8272 and taken into stock the following year. She has given 26 years of loyal service; 2 March 1968.

[A. Wilkinson]

All the signs of a rearguard stand, valiantly fought without hope and against overwhelming odds; layers of oil and brake block dust caked on wheels and motion contrast sharply with the days of large cleaning gangs and immaculate locomotives.

[A. Wilkinson]

The Changing of the Guard; Old warrior and new commando stand at ease together on the last day of steam at Northwich. 48036 (VF36) awaits its final turn of duty on the Winnington tripper, and D5277 lays over between workings on the limestone hoppers to Peak Forest; 2 March 1968. During the year steam hauled trains of every sort began to merit attention in view of the imminence of their almost unbelievable disappearance.   [A. Wilkinson]

The climb over Copy Pit, approached from either side by 1 in 60 gradients, was briefly rediscovered as a new Shap. This was a fine scenic route and merited greater attention than it had received previously. On a fine summer morning 48765 (Dn46) works hard on the climb near Cliviger with a mixed freight from Burnley to Healey Mills, assisted by 48167 (C43) banking in reverse. A more recent suggestion that this was a rare sighting of the experimental 8F prototype HST—Interfreight 65—may be categorically denied, and should perhaps be treated with caution . . . 19 July 1968.　　　　　[M. Mitchell]

The rugged industrial landscape and gritstone scarps of Rossendale became steam's last hun ground; 48773 hurries the SVRS/MRTS 'Farewell to Steam' special away from Todmorde the beginning of the last week of steam, 26 July 1968.　　　　　[D. E. Gouldtho

By July 1968 steam working was confined to Carnforth, Lostock Hall and Rose Grove, and the area covered by these depots saw an enthusiast invasion of quite unprecedented proportions. With three days of service left, 48773 (NBL40) blows off furiously nearing Rose Grove with the 18.50 Preston–Healey Mills express fitted freight: subsequently. this 40 wagon train was taken over Copy Pit unassisted; 31 July 1968.

[M. Taylor]

Some enthusiasts, for whom armchair nostalgia was an inadequate, negative outlet, have cleaned 48666 (B44) which has lost its top feed casing at some point—a 'last week' scene at Rose Grove. In the background withdrawn members of the class await the inevitable journey to oblivion.   [J. B. Caldwell]

48191 (NBL42) was the last Copy Pit banker. Embellishments chalked on her smokebox door proclaim the 'gricers' lament to the days of 'thrash, clag and noise' now ended, 3 August 1968.

[Norman Preedy]

TCDD 45156 (NBL40) at Sivas depot in Turkey, on 29 September 1976, was originally ordered as W D 346. A? engines destined for Turkey were constructed with, or altered to, left hand drive. The footplate valance, m? bracket and some motion parts are picked out in red, shown here by their lighter appearance. This engine retains her original smokebox door. The water column conceals a cast metal star and crescent insignia on the te? side. It is good to see her still in service after 35 years' use: long may she steam, even on the coal slack the T? appear to use!

[A. K. Ga?

On shed at Ulukisla, Turkey, on 6 August 1974, TCDD 45167 (NBL40) sports a replacement smokebox door but retains her original builder's plate. As related earlier—the Turks were permitted to buy 27 Stanier 2-8-0s in the early years of the war, and this locomotive, built as WD 352, was allocated for export to Turkey either while under construction or when just completed. Twenty-five engines were sent out in 1941, of which seven were lost at sea, and two more were delivered in 1943.

[T. E. Talbot]

48773 was purchased from BR in 1968 by the Stanier 8F Locomotive Society, and restored in her earlier guise as LMS 8233: she now enjoys a new lease of life on the Severn Valley Railway. In the early morning of 23 April 1977 she crosses Oldbury Viaduct with the SVR railtour set that has been restored in GW livery and passed for BR mainline running. 8233 will come off at Bewdley, but the train will travel behind two more preserved locomotives, GWR 6000 *King George V* and LMS 6201 *Princess Elizabeth* on different stages of the round trip to Chester.

[A. Wilkinson]

48431 was rescued from Barry scrapyard for restoration in 1971 and now operates on the Keighley & Worth Valley Railway; this was one of the engines fitted with the larger forward-mounted ejector. She is seen double-heading W D 2-8-0 1931 on a train from Keighley to Oxenhope in 1975. The W D engine, a wartime derivative of the Stanier design, acquired a new cab among other modifications carried out to fit her for working north of the Arctic Circle while languishing in Sweden before purchase for preservation in 1974. [R. Higgins]

The Stockton & Darlington Railway 150th Anniversary celebrations brought together an impressive display of reserved steam power, much of it now owned privately: 8233, 43106 and coaches from the S V R leave York for Darlington on 11 August 1975. [J. R. P. Hunt]

Built as WD 307 (NBL40), and operating successively as LMS 8233, ISR 41.109, WD 70307, WD 500 and BR 48773, until finally restored as LMS 8233, this widely travelled locomotive recaptures the past with the 10.30 Bridgnorth–Bewdley special freight on 18 September 1975. Together with LMS 8431, she remains a working reminder of a stalwart and distinguished locomotive class.

[J. R. P. Hunt]

Acknowledgements

The editors and publishers wish to thank the many photographers whose work appears in this volume and without whom it could not have been compiled. Thanks must also be recorded to the following for equally valuable assistance in other respects: Major R. J. Wade, RE (retd.); Colonel G. C. L. Alexander, O.B.E., T.D., late RE (retd.); Major W. Kirby, G.M., RE (retd.); Mr. D. S. Currie; Mr. E. A. Langridge; Mr. V. Forster; Mr. J. H. Russell; Mr. J. W. P. Rowledge; Mr. D. C. Williams; and Mr. B. D. Palmer.

MIDLAND
NORTH OF THE BORDER
NORTH EASTERN
STEAM
GREAT WESTERN
STEAM MISCELLANY
BODMIN AND WADEBRIDGE
STANDARD STEAM
IN ACTION
BRITISH
NARROW GAUGE
STEAM
A PICTORIAL SURVEY
GREAT WESTERN
BRANCH LINE STEAM 2
DIESELS
ON SCOTTISH REGION
BR DIESELS
IN ACTION
H.C.CASSERLEY
IRISH RAILWAYS
in the heyday of steam
SOUTHERN
188
THE LYNTON & BARNSTAPLE RAILWAY
THE WARSHIPS
THE WAINWRIGHT CLASSES
STEAM
LONDON MIDLAND
STEAM IN ACTION 4
42/43 DIESEL-HYDRAULICS
NORTH EASTERN
STEAM
LONDON RT BUS
STANIER 8F
2-8-0
STEAM
GREAT CENTRAL
recalled